STOIC WISDOM

QUOTES, AFFIRMATION,

AND INSPIRATION

FOR A WELL-LIVED LIFE

chartwell
books

INTRODUCTION

What is a well-lived life?

THIS QUESTION PREOCCUPIED THE GREAT THINKERS who developed the philosophy of Stoicism more than 2,000 years ago. Inspired by earlier philosophers including Socrates and the Cynics, the Stoics developed theories of logic, physics, and ethics, pondering the biggest questions we confront as humans. What is the meaning of life? What is our relationship to nature? What is the best way to live?

Because the divine exists in nature, they reasoned, nature is perfectly ordered. Each part of the universe has a purpose, including ourselves. Each of us can achieve *eudaimonia*, translated as "happiness" or "flourishing," by living in accordance with that which is in our nature. But how do we do that? Applying reason, achieving virtue, seeking wisdom and justice, and practicing temperament are all essential to a flourishing life. Resisting that which disturbs or distresses our souls, focusing on what we can control, and doing our duty are part of it, too.

Through their writing, the Stoics offered wisdom for helping anyone hoping to become the best version of themselves. Greek-born Roman philosopher Epictetus offered *Discourses*, discussing how adversity makes us stronger and how we can adapt a more neutral posture toward situations and people that cause us distress. In his *Letters to Lucilus*, Seneca proposes how we should approach the time we are given on Earth: with gratitude, in community, and with inner peace. In his *Meditations*, Roman emperor and philosopher Marcus Aurelius reminds us that life is short and there is nothing that we can control but our own thoughts and feelings and how we react to life's circumstances. To be humble, patient, empathetic, and generous is not easy. But if we can master ourselves, these virtues are within our reach.

The wise words of these ancient philosophers are more powerful than ever today. In our hectic and materialistic world with its endless distractions, there is no shortage of opportunities to look outward for guidance. But the Stoics taught us that everything we need to achieve a flourishing life already exists within us. We just need to cultivate it. In this beautifully illustrated volume, the words of the ancients reach out to you across the centuries, providing guidance and inspiration. The deep truths of the Stoics can help you in your day-to-day life, providing touchstones that remind you of your own inner resources. You will return time and again to these enduring words of advice, each time finding meaning, solace, and direction.

Stoic Wisdom is a contemplative way to encounter the words of the Stoics. As you leaf through the pages, let the words and images soak in, leaving a profound impact on you. You will remember the lessons you learn from these great thinkers as you encounter difficulties, reflect on your approach to life and relationships, and plot your future. There has never been a better time to apply the insight of the Stoics than today. Connect with this age-old wisdom and build it into your own mindfulness and self-actualization practices.

THE STOIC PHILOSOPHERS

Heraclitus

Around 500 BCE
Pre-Stoic Greek Socratic philosopher; inspired the Stoics

Heraclitus is remembered for his theories on change, known as the Doctrine of Flux, as well as the Unity of Opposites, the idea that the existence of a thing is dependent on the existence of an opposite, contained within a harmonious universe.

Cleanthes

Around 330 BCE–Unknown
Follower of Zeno who became the second leader of the Stoic School of Athens

Cleanthes developed the idea of Stoic physics, the theory of how all parts of the universe work together.

500 BCE | 400 BCE | 300 BCE | 200 BCE

Zeno of Citium

Around 334–262 BCE
Greek Philosopher, Considered the Father of Stoicism

Zeno developed the concept of dialectic or reasoned discussion, contributing not only to philosophy but physics and ethics.

Chrysippus

Around 279–206 BCE
Student of Cleanthes who became leader of the Stoic School of Athens

Known for his theory of knowledge, ethics, and physics, Chrysippus developed a system of propositional logic.

Cato the Younger

Around 95 BCE–46 BCE
Roman Senator and Philosopher

A proponent of traditional Roman values, he was banished by Caesar.

Seneca

(Lucius Annaeus Seneca the Younger)
Around 4 BCE–65 CE
Roman philosopher

A prolific writer, his work was revived by many Renaissance writers and philosophers.

Musonius Rufus

25 CE–95 CE
Roman Stoic exiled by Nero

An advocate for living a simple life, he was the tutor of Epictetus.

100 BCE | 0 CE | 100 CE | 200 CE

Diogenes of Babylon

Around 230–140 BCE
Greek Philosopher, later leader of the Stoic School of Athens

Both a Cynic and early Stoic, He was known for bringing Stoicism to Rome.

Epictetus

Around 50–135 CE
Greek-born Roman philosopher born into slavery

Known for his discourses on self-control and acceptance of fate, he is considered among the most influential of the Stoics.

Marcus Aurelius

121–180 CE
***Roman emperor and philosopher known for his* Meditations**

Emperor of Rome during a turbulent time, he wrote some of the most influential philosophy texts in history.

When you arise
in the morning,
think of what a
precious privilege
it is to be alive—to
breathe, to think,
to enjoy, to love.

MARCUS AURELIUS

We cannot choose our
external circumstances,
but we can always choose
how we respond to them.

EPICTETUS

Everyone has the
gift of speech.
But few have the
gift of wisdom.

CATO THE YOUNGER

TO LEARN WHAT

HE ALREADY

EPICTETUS

HE THINKS KNOWS.

ἀμήχανον γάρ, ἅ τις εἰδέναι οἴεται,
ταῦτα ἄρξασθαι μανθάνειν.

As long
as you
live, keep
learning
how to live.

SENECA

Man conquers the world by conquering himself.
ZENO OF CITIUM

Zeno of Citium

ZENO WAS BORN AROUND 334 BCE IN CITIUM on the island of Cyprus. After a successful career as a merchant, he ended up in Athens and became a student of the Cynic philosopher Crates. Under Crates, he developed his own philosophy and began teaching on the Stoa Poikile (Painted Porch). His philosophy came to be known as Stoicism.

Zeno believed that nature (the universe) was rational and, therefore, to live in accordance with nature was to live the best possible life. In order to do so, he taught, we must not be slaves to our passions. Instead, we must develop *apatheia*, a state of detachment and nonjudgment from our thoughts and feelings. We should not wish for a trouble-free life, he said, because difficulties help us to build virtue and character.

Zeno's Stoic School of Athens continued after his death, led by those who ascribed to his views. Although none of Zeno's works survived intact, we know of his teachings because of the fragments stated and quoted by those who followed him.

Small-minded
people blame others.
Average people
blame themselves.
The wise see all
blame as foolishness.

EPICTETUS

We have two ears
and one mouth, so
we should listen
more than we say.

ZENO OF CITIUM

THE IMPEDIMENT
ADVANCES
STANDS IN THE
THE WAY.

MARCUS AURELIUS

TO ACTION ACTION. WHAT WAY BECOMES

Quod obstat viae fit via.

No man is more unhappy than he who never faces adversity. For he is not permitted to prove himself.

SENECA

Everyone has the gift of speech. But few have the gift of wisdom.

CATO THE YOUNGER

If you are distressed by anything external, the pain is not due to the thing itself, but to your estimate of it; and this you have the power to revoke at any moment.

MARCUS AURELIUS

Cleanthes

CLEANTHES WAS BORN AROUND 330 BCE IN ASSOS, a city in what's now Turkey. He worked as a pugilist (boxer) to support himself financially while studying philosophy. Cleanthes studied under Zeno, the founder of Stoicism, and became one of his most prominent students, taking over from him as the head of the Stoic School in Athens.

Cleanthes is best known for formalizing the Stoic philosophy after Zeno's death. He is credited with numerous works, although few of his original writings have survived. In particular, he is said to have written extensively on Stoic physics and the Stoic concept of the logos (the rational principle governing the universe).

One of Cleanthes' few surviving works is *Hymn to Zeus*, a poetic prayer expressing Stoic beliefs about the nature of the divine and the interconnectedness of all things. This hymn reflects Cleanthes' deep reverence for the rational order of the cosmos and his conviction that human beings should live in harmony with nature.

Cleanthes served as the head of the Stoic School in Athens until his death around 230 BCE. He was succeeded by his famous student, Chrysippus, who further developed and expanded Stoic philosophy.

You always own the option of having no opinion. There is never any need to get worked up or to trouble your soul about things you can't control. These things are not asking to be judged by you. Leave them alone.

MARCUS AURELIUS

Nothing is more honorable than a grateful heart.

SENECA

ADAPT YOURSELF TO
IN WHICH YOUR LOT
AND SHOW TRUE
FELLOW-MORTALS
HAS SURROUNDED

MARCUS AURELIUS

THE ENVIRONMENT HAS BEEN CAST, LOVE TO THE WITH WHOM DESTINY YoU.

Οἷς συγκεκλήρωσαι πράγμασι,
τούτοις συνάρμοζε σεαυτόν,
καὶ οἷς συνείληχας ἀνθρώποις,
τούτους φίλει, ἀλλ ἀληθινῶς.

The soul is dyed the color of its thoughts. Think only on those things that are in line with your principles and can bear the light of day. The content of your character is your choice. Day by day, what you do is who you become. Your integrity is your destiny—it is the light that guides your way.

HERACLITUS

FIRE IS THE TEST OF GOLD; ADVERSITY, OF STRONG MEN.

SENECA

TEST OF ADVERSITY, MEN.

Ignis aurum probat,
miseria fortes viros.

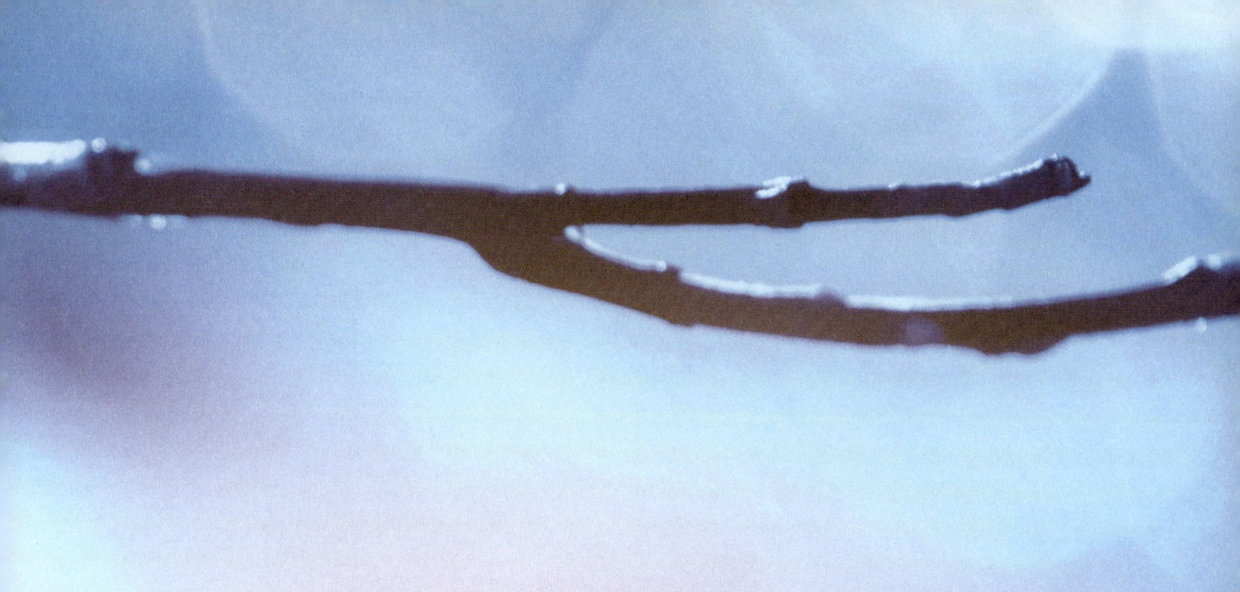

You become what you give your attention to.

EPICTETUS

Do not try to seem wise to others. If you want to live a wise life, live it on your own terms and in your own eyes.

EPICTETUS

You don't love yourself enough. Or you'd love your nature, too, and what it demands of you.

MARCUS AURELIUS

Seneca

LUCIUS ANNAEUS SENECA WAS BORN AROUND 65 BCE in the Roman colony of Corduba, now Cordoba, Spain. He moved to Rome as a young boy and studied oration and philosophy. Due to an illness, he went to live in Egypt with his aunt and uncle. At age 31, he returned to Rome and began his political career. When he ran afoul of the emperor Caligula, he used his philosophical and rhetorical skills to argue his way out of an execution. Instead, he was banished. Later, he was able to return to Rome and served in the senate. He tutored the emperor Nero, who also later tried to have him executed.

Most of his important work was written after he retired. His famous works include *Letters to Lucilius*, and the treatises *On Anger, On Mercy, On Leisure, On the Constancy of the Wise Person, On Providence*, and *On Benefits*. He is now considered to have been one of the greatest intellectuals of the Roman empire.

If it is not right, do not do it; if it is not true, do not say it.

MARCUS AURELIUS

Wealth
consists not in
having great
possessions,
but in having
few wants.

EPICTETUS

An angry man
opens his mouth
and shuts his eyes.

CATO THE YOUNGER

No loss should
be more
regrettable to
us than losing
our time, for it's
irretrievable.

ZENO OF CITIUM

Never esteem anything as of advantage to you that will make you break your word or lose your self-respect.

MARCUS AURELIUS

FIRST SAY TO
WHAT YOU
AND THEN
HAVE TO DO.

EPICTETUS

YOURSELF
WOULD BE;
DO WHAT YOU

Τίς εἶναι θέλεις, σαυτῷ πρῶτον
εἰπέ: εἶθ' οὕτως ποίει ἃ ποιεῖς.

If you want to improve, be content to be thought foolish and stupid.

EPICTETUS

All things are parts
of one single system,
which is called nature;
the individual life is
good when it is in
harmony with nature.

ZENO OF CITIUM

STOIC SPOTLIGHT

Marcus Aurelius

MARCUS AURELIUS IS CONSIDERED one of the most important Stoics. Born into a prominent political family in Rome in 121 CE, he was interested in philosophy from a young age. Two of his tutors were Stoics, and he was especially interested in the *Discourses* of Epictetus, the Greek philosopher and former slave. He entered a life of politics when he was adopted into the imperial family, and in 161 CE was named as co-emperor along with his brother Lucius Verus, who later died in a pandemic.

Although power, wealth, and prestige were of paramount importance in his world, Marcus Aurelius viewed everything through the Stoic framework, so he didn't value these things. He ruled during very turbulent times, and his emphasis on virtue and duty marked his time in power. Although his most famous work, *Meditations*, illustrates the time he devoted to reflection, he also spent most of his time on the battlefield, which is where he died in 180 CE. *Meditations* is one of the key texts of Stoicism, offering wisdom that's been embraced for thousands of years.

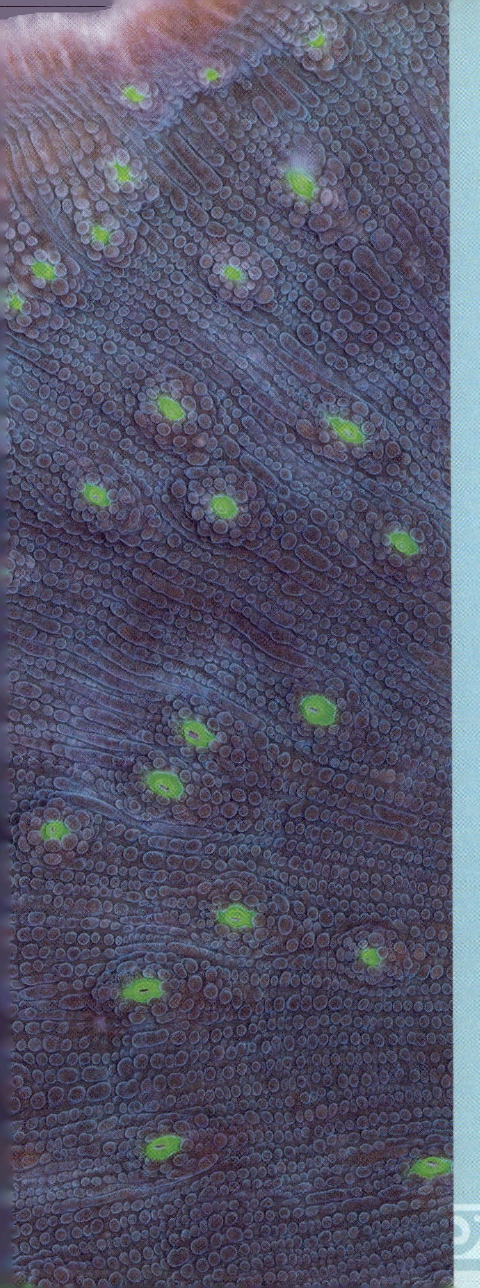

How ridiculous and how strange to be surprised at anything which happens in life.

MARCUS AURELIUS

IF IT IS
THEN ENDURE
DON'T

MARCUS AURELIUS

ENDURABLE,
IT AND
COMPLAIN.

εἰ μὲν οὖν συμβαίνει σοι, ὡς πέφυκας φέρειν, μὴ δυσχέραινε· ἀλλ᾽ ὡς πέφυκας, φέρε.

It's not what
happens to you,
but how you react
to it that matters.

EPICTETUS

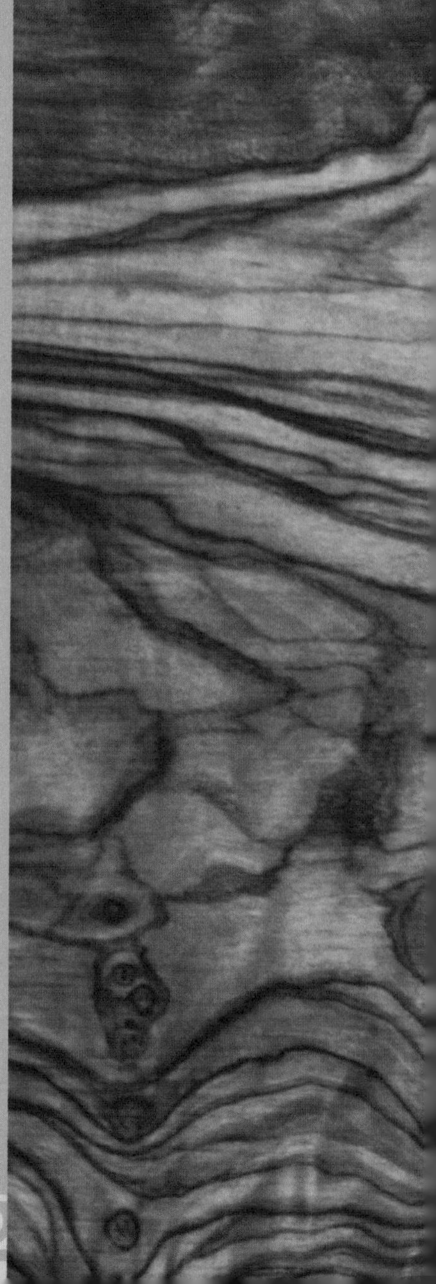

If what you have seems insufficient to you, then though you possess the world, you will yet be miserable.

SENECA

Never depend on the admiration of others. There is no strength in it. Personal merit cannot be derived from an external source. It is not to be found in your personal associations, nor can it be found in the regard of other people. It is a fact of life that other people, even people who love you, will not necessarily agree with your ideas, understand you, or share your enthusiasms. Grow up! Who cares what other people think about you!

EPICTETUS

YOUR DAYS ARE
THEM TO THROW
OF YOUR SOUL TO
NOT, THE SUN
AND YOU WITH IT

EPICTETUS

NUMBERED. USE
OPEN THE WINDOWS
THE SUN. IF YOU DO
WILL SOON SET,

ὅρος ἐστί σοι περιγεγραμμένος
τοῦ χρόνου, ᾧ ἐὰν εἰς τὸ
ἀπαιθριάσαι μὴ χρήσῃ, οἰχήσεται
καὶ οἰχήσῃ καὶ αὖθις οὐκ ἐξέσται.

No man can have
a peaceful life who
thinks too much
about lengthening it.

SENECA

Do not waste what remains of your life in speculating about your neighbors, unless with a view to some mutual benefit. To wonder what so-and-so is doing and why, or what he is saying, or thinking, or scheming—in a word, anything that distracts you from fidelity to the ruler within you—means a loss of opportunity for some other task.

MARCUS AURELIUS

THE BEST IS TO BE HE WHO THE

MARCUS AURELIUS

REVENGE UNLIKE CAUSED INJURY.

εἰ μὲν οὖν συμβαίνει σοι, ὡς πέφυκας φέρειν, μὴ δυσχέραινε· ἀλλ᾽ ὡς πέφυκας, φέρε.

Choose not to be harmed, and you won't feel harmed. Don't feel harmed, and you haven't been.

MARCUS AURELIUS

Difficulties strengthen the mind, as labor does the body.

SENECA

The key is to keep company only with people who uplift you, whose presence calls forth your best.

EPICTETUS

No man ever steps in the same river twice, for it's not the same river and he's not the same man.

HERACLITUS

Epictetus

EPICTETUS BORN AROUND 55 BCE IN THE CITY OF HIERAPOLIS, located in modern-day Turkey. He grew up as a slave and was taken to Rome to serve Epaphroditus, who formerly served as a slave for emperor Nero. While still a slave, he had the chance to study philosophy under Musonius Rufus. He later gained his freedom and began to teach Stoicism.

Epictetus' major contribution to Stoicism was around the Dichotomy of Control, which he wrote about in his *Discourses*. This theory asserted that inner peace can only be achieved through understanding and accepting what we can and can't control. He believed that freedom comes from within, through mastery of one's own desires and emotions. In addition to *Discourses, Enchiridion* is another of his most famous works. Epictetus influenced all Roman Stoics who came after him, most notably Marcus Aurelius.

Frightened of change? But what can exist without it? What's closer to nature's heart? Can you take a hot bath and leave the firewood as it was? Eat food without transforming it? Can any vital process take place without something being changed? Can't you see? It's just the same with you–and just as vital to nature.

MARCUS AURELIUS

Those who are well constituted in the body endure both heat and cold: and so those who are well constituted in the soul endure both anger and grief and excessive joy and the other affects.

EPICTETUS

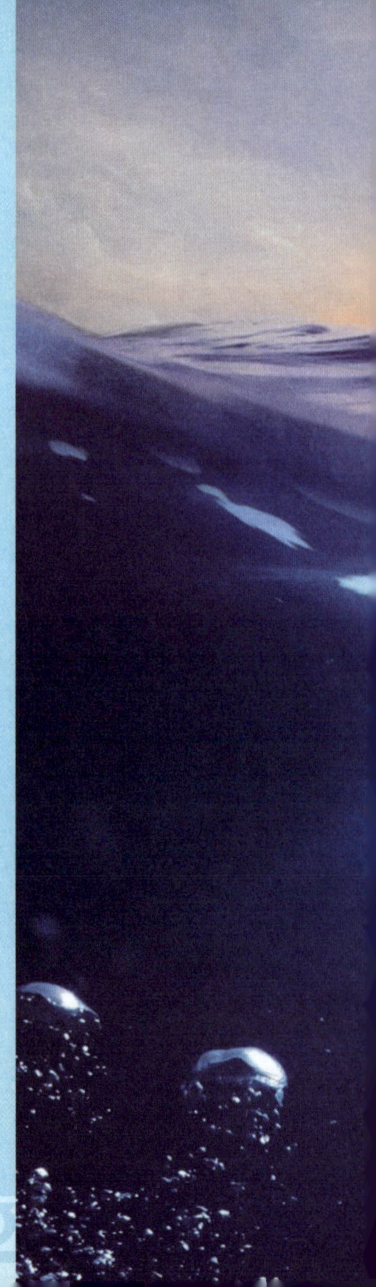

The happiness of those who want to be popular depends on others; the happiness of those who seek pleasure fluctuates with moods outside their control; but the happiness of the wise grows out of their own free acts.

MARCUS AURELIUS

Let us say what we feel and feel what we say; let speech harmonize with life.

SENECA

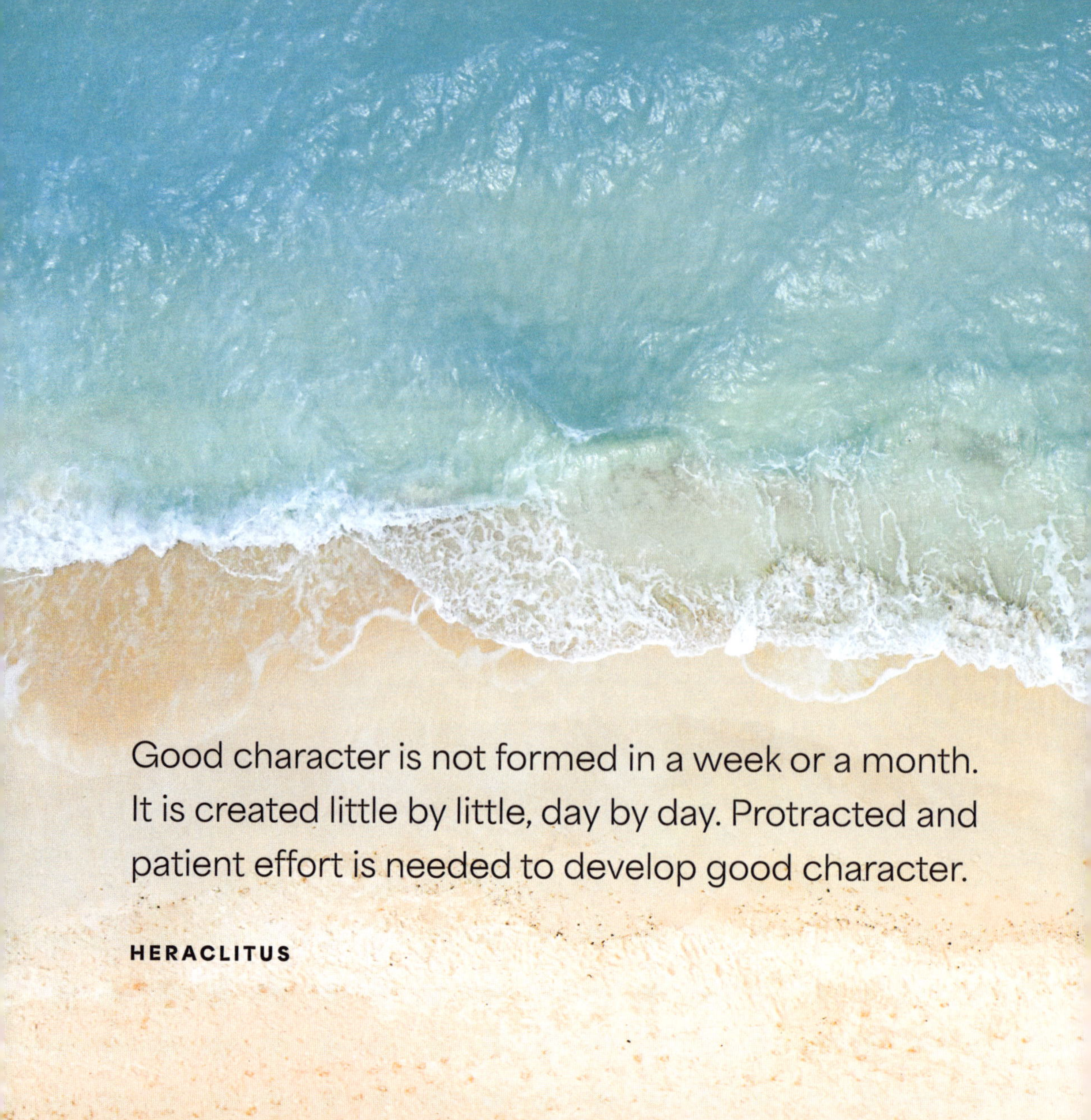

Good character is not formed in a week or a month. It is created little by little, day by day. Protracted and patient effort is needed to develop good character.

HERACLITUS

To accept injury without a spirit of savage resentment—to show ourselves merciful toward those who wrong us—being a source of good hope to them—is characteristic of a benevolent and civilized way of life.

MUSONIUS RUFUS

Dwell on the
beauty of life.
Watch the stars
and see yourself
running with them.

MARCUS AURELIUS

Happiness is a good flow of life.

ZENO OF CITIUM

At dawn, when you have trouble getting out of bed, tell yourself: "I have to go to work–as a human being. What do I have to complain of, if I'm going to do what I was born for–the things I was brought into the world to do? Or is this what I was created for? To huddle under the blankets and stay warm?

MARCUS AURELIUS

Gauis Musonius Rufus

BORN AROUND 30 BC IN VOLSINII, a Roman city located in what's now the Italian city of Orvieto, Gaius Musonius Rufus became known as a great Stoic teacher. He didn't limit his teaching to men, which was quite revolutionary at the time. His most famous student was Epictetus.

Musonius Rufus was known for his commitment to virtue and to a simple life, including eating a vegetarian diet, maintaining one's physical health, dressing simply, and eschewing luxury. He believed that an austere lifestyle prepared people for the inevitable hardships that life presents. He stressed marital fidelity and stability in relationships. He advocated for large families, believing this was in accordance with nature. In his rhetorical style, he emphasized not showing off or trying to appear clever, but centering on virtue.

Only a few of his quotes and longer discourses have survived, but they are frequently referenced by other philosophers who were his students or who were inspired by him.

Do not indulge in dreams of having what you have not, but reckon up the chief of the blessings you do possess, and then thankfully remember how you would crave for them if they were not yours.

MARCUS AURELIUS

I judge you unfortunate because you have never lived through misfortune. You have passed through life without an opponent—no one can ever know what you are capable of, not even you.

SENECA

Caretake this moment. Immerse yourself in its particulars. Respond to this person, this challenge, this deed. Quit evasions. Stop giving yourself needless trouble. It is time to really live; to fully inhabit the situation you happen to be

EPICTETUS

A MAN'S DELIGHT IS HE WAS

MARCUS AURELIUS

TRUE
TO DO THINGS
MADE FOR.

Vera delectatio hominis est
facere quod creatus est

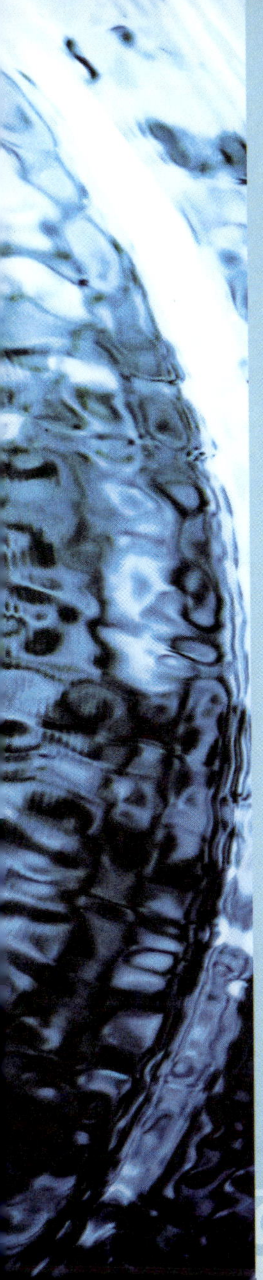

All you need are these:
certainty of judgment in the
present moment; action for
the common good in the
present moment; and an
attitude of gratitude in
the present moment for
anything that comes your way.

MARCUS AURELIUS

Accept the things to which fate binds you, and love the people with whom fate brings you together, but do so with all your heart.

EPICTETUS

No man is hurt but by himself. ...Literally, by how he interprets what happens to him. If he focuses on how it could have been better, he will be hurt. If he focuses on how it could have been worse, he will be happy. The same is true for women, too.

DIOGENES OF BABYLON

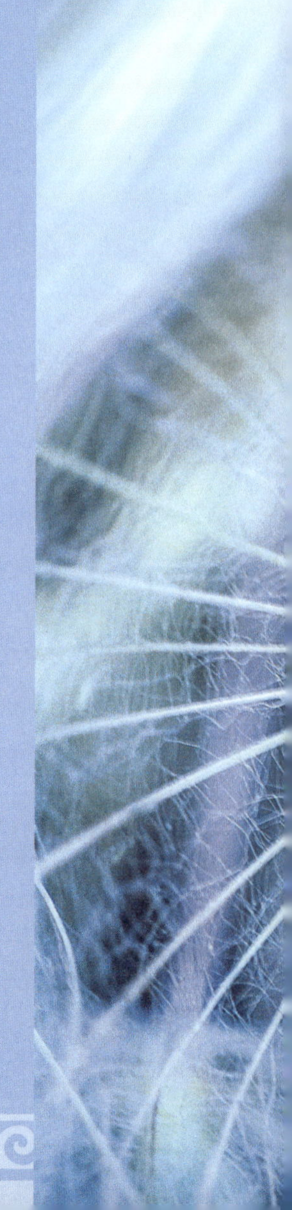

Think of all the years passed by in which you said to yourself "I'll do it tomorrow," and how the gods have again and again granted you periods of grace of which you have not availed yourself. It is time to realize that you are a member of the Universe, that you are born of Nature itself, and to know that a limit has been set to your time. Use every moment wisely, to perceive your inner refulgence, or 'twill be gone and nevermore within your reach.

MARCUS AURELIUS

HOW LONG GOING TO BEFORE YOU BEST FOR

EPICTETUS

ARE YOU WAIT DEMAND THE YOURSELF?

εἰς ποῖον ἔτι χρόνον
ἀναβάλλῃ τὸ τῶν βελτίστων
ἀξιοῦν σεαυτὸν.

To accept injury without a spirit of savage resentment—to show ourselves merciful toward those who wrong us—being a source of good hope to them—is characteristic of a benevolent and civilized way of life.

MUSONIUS RUFUS

The willing are led
by fate, the reluctant
are dragged.

CLEANTHES

Cato the Younger

CATO THE YOUNGER, ALSO KNOWN as Marcus Porcius Cato, was born into a wealthy Roman family in 95 BCE. Growing up, he was educated in philosophy and studied the Stoics, but ended up entering politics instead. He held many bureaucratic and political roles before eventually reaching the rank of senator. Throughout his career, he was a champion of the common people. He helped create a public library. But he made himself an enemy of Julius Caesar, of whom he was openly critical.

Cato was a fierce defender of Roman traditions. He was known for his Spartan lifestyle: he walked everywhere instead of riding, was often barefoot, and wore a simple toga. He believed his choices to be symbolic of Roman virtue. When his feud with Caesar escalated, he was forced to leave the Empire and ultimately fled to what's now North Africa.

Cato is known primarily for writing *Origins*, which is about the history of Rome and *On Farming*. Most of what we know about him comes from his contemporaries or writers who sought to memorialize him.

To love only what happens, what was destined. No greater harmony.

MARCUS AURELIUS

Growing old is not so bad when you consider the alternative.

CATO THE YOUNGER

Wise people are in want of nothing, and yet need many things. On the other hand, nothing is needed by fools, for they do not understand how to use anything, but are in want of everything.

CHRYSIPPUS

Neither should a ship rely on one small anchor, nor should life rest on a single hope.

EPICTETUS

Think of the life you have lived until now as over and, as a dead man, see what's left as a bonus and live it according to Nature. Love the hand that fate deals you and play it as your own, for what could be more fitting?

MARCUS AURELIUS

There is only one way to happiness and that is to cease worrying about things which are beyond the power of our will.

EPICTETUS

It is not because things are difficult that we do not dare, it is because we do not dare that they are difficult.

SENECA

Curb your desire—don't set your heart on so many things and you will get what you need.

EPICTETUS

STOIC SPOTLIGHT

Chrysippus

CHRYSIPPUS WAS BORN AROUND 279 BCE in Cilicia in what is now Turkey. He moved to Athens when he was young and began studying with Cleanthes at the Stoic School.

Chrysippus developed the concept of propositional logic; that is, the idea that a statement can be true or false, but it can't be both. He helped advance the importance of living in accordance with nature and cultivating virtue as the key to *eudaimonia*, or flourishing. He believed that happiness and tranquility could be attained through the practice of virtue and the acceptance of fate.

Chrysippus also furthered the idea of Stoic physics, the branch of Stoicism that seeks to understand the way the universe works. He also developed a theory of determinism; that is, the idea that all events are determined by the laws of nature.

Although it's believed that he wrote over 700 books, much of Chrysippus's writing has been lost to time, with only a few passages remaining.

Quarto

This edition was published in 2024 by Chartwell Books,
an imprint of The Quarto Group
142 West 36th Street, 4th Floor
New York, NY 10018 USA
T (212) 779-4972 F (212) 779-6058
www.Quarto.com

10 9 8 7 6 5 4 3 2 1

Chartwell titles are also available at discount for retail, wholesale, promotional, and bulk purchase. For details, contact the Special Sales Manager by email at specialsales@quarto.com or by mail at The Quarto Group, Attn: Special Sales Manager, 100 Cummings Center Suite 265D, Beverly, MA 01915, USA.

ISBN: 978-0-7858-4656-7

Publisher: Wendy Friedman
Publishing Director: Meredith Mennitt
Editor: Joanne O'Sullivan
Designer: Sue Boylan
Image credits: Shutterstock

Printed in China